"HOLD HIM DOWN"
(SELF-HELP) GUIDE TO A SUCCESSFUL RELATIONSHIP

OTIS JACKSON SR

FIRST KLASS PUBLISHING

I dedicate this book to my mother Vivian Jackson this one for you !!!!!!!! Special shoutout to my kids and fiance' Daryen Baugh who put up with my late nights while trying to complete my mission.

"WE ARE ALL FOOLS IN LOVE"

                                  -JANE AUSTEN

CONTENTS

Title Page

Dedication

Epigraph

Introduction

Prologue

Chapter 1 : Communication - The Foundation of a Healthy Relationship … 1

Chapter 2: Trust and Honesty - The Glue That Holds the Relationship Together … 3

Chapter 3: Emotional Intelligence - Understanding and Managing Your Emotions … 6

Chapter 4: Support and Encouragement - Being a Rock for Your Partner … 10

Chapter 5: Intimacy and Connection - Building a Strong Physical and Emotional Bond … 18

Chapter 6: Independence and Interdependence - Finding a Healthy Balance … 23

Chapter 7: Conflict and Resolution - Addressing Conflicts in a Healthy and Constructive Manner … 27

Chapter 8: Personal Growth and Development - Continuing to Grow and Evolve as Individuals … 32

Acknowledgement … 37

Afterword	41
About The Author	43

INTRODUCTION

Building a healthy relationship takes effort and commitment from both partners. It requires communication, trust, and mutual respect to create a strong bond that can withstand life's challenges. In this eBook, we'll explore the key components of a successful relationship and provide practical tips on how to keep a man happy, fulfilled, and committed.

Prologue

In a world where the dynamics of relationships are ever-evolving, there exists a profound for understanding and gentle love from the female perspective. Mr. Jackson has harvested a deep insight into the intricate dance of keeping a man satisfied and content in a relationship. Through his own experiences and wisdom gained, he unveils the principles and practices in his book "HOLD HIM DOWN" as a guide to keeping a man happy

With empathy and clarity, The author delves into the nuances of communication, emotional intimacy, and mutual respect that lay the foundation for a thriving partnership. As the pages of this book unfold, readers are guided on a transformative journey towards cultivating a harmonious bond with thier partners.

"HOLD HIM DOWN" is not just a guidebook; it is a beacon of light for women seeking to navigate the complexities of love with grace and wisdom. Join Mr. Jackson as he shares the keys to unlocking the secrets of lasting happiness in a relationship, empowering women to create enduring connections that stand the test of time.

CHAPTER 1 : COMMUNICATION - THE FOUNDATION OF A HEALTHY RELATIONSHIP

Communication is the bedrock of any successful relationship, serving as the catalyst for understanding, connection, and growth between partners. It encompasses more than just words; it is an unique gesture of active listening, emotional transparency, and empathy that nurtures intimacy and trust. In this chapter, we explore the transformative power of effective communication in fostering a resilient and fulfilling relationship.

Key Points:

1. **Active Listening:** Engage with your partner's words, emotions, and unspoken messages to create a safe space for vulnerability and authentic connection.

2. **Emotional Transparency:** Be open and honest about your thoughts, feelings, and needs to build trust and mutual respect within the relationship.

3. **Navigating Conflict:** Approach conflicts with compassion, empathy, and a willingness to find common ground and solutions together.

4. **Non-Verbal Communication:** Pay attention to body language, facial expressions, and gestures to deepen mutual understanding and reinforce emotional connection.

5. **Empathy and Understanding:** Cultivate empathy by stepping into your partner's shoes, validating their experiences, and prioritizing mutual understanding in communication.

6. **Love Languages:** Recognize and honor your partner's love language to enhance intimacy, strengthen emotional bonds, and foster a sense of connection and fulfillment.

Effective communication is a continuous journey of growth, learning, and adaptation. By prioritizing open, honest, and empathetic communication, partners lay a solid foundation for resilience, intimacy, and shared happiness in their relationship. Embrace the transformative power of communication as a profound expression of love, respect, and shared vulnerability, enriching the journey of partnership together.

Communication is the backbone of any successful relationship. It's the key to understanding each other's needs, desires, and emotions. Without effective communication, misunderstandings and conflicts can arise, leading to a breakdown in the relationship. In this chapter, we'll explore the different types of communication, how to practice active listening, and how to express yourself clearly and assertively.

△△△

CHAPTER 2: TRUST AND HONESTY - THE GLUE THAT HOLDS THE RELATIONSHIP TOGETHER

In the complex detail of relationships, trust and honesty stand as the pillars that uphold the foundation of a strong and enduring bond between partners. They serve as the glue that binds hearts, minds, and souls, fostering a sense of security, intimacy, and authenticity within the relationship. In this chapter, we delve into the profound significance of trust and honesty, exploring their transformative power in nurturing a deep and meaningful connection.

The Essence of Trust:

Trust is the bedrock upon which the seeds of love and intimacy flourish, weaving a web of security and reliability between partners. It is the unwavering belief in one another's integrity, intentions, and faithfulness, creating a safe space where vulnerabilities can be shared and cherished. Trust is not given lightly; it is earned through consistent actions, transparency, and a commitment to mutual respect and understanding.

The Importance of Honesty:

Honesty serves as the guiding light that illuminates the path to authenticity and vulnerability in a relationship. It is the courage to speak your truth, share your fears, and express your desires openly and sincerely. Honesty nurtures a culture of transparency and accountability, fostering a sense of emotional safety and acceptance between partners. It is through honesty that trust deepens, walls crumble, and hearts intertwine in a dance of shared truth and connection.

Building a Foundation of Trust:

Trust is nurtured through consistent actions that align with words, intentions, and values. It requires open communication, active listening, and a willingness to be vulnerable with one another. Building trust entails showing up for your partner, honoring your commitments, and respecting boundaries and agreements within the relationship. It is a continuous process of cultivating emotional safety, reliability, and respect that forms the cornerstone of a healthy and thriving connection.

The Role of Honesty in Communication:

Honesty in communication involves more than just speaking the truth; it encompasses active listening, empathy, and a willingness to engage in difficult conversations with respect and compassion. It involves being authentic about your feelings, needs, and boundaries, and creating a space where both partners feel seen, heard, and valued. Honesty fosters intimacy, deepens emotional connection, and nurtures a sense of mutual understanding and acceptance within the relationship.

Rebuilding Trust After Betrayal:

Trust, once broken, can be a fragile entity that requires time, patience, and effort to rebuild. It demands introspection, accountability, and a willingness to acknowledge past mistakes and hurts. Rebuilding trust after betrayal involves open dialogue, genuine remorse, and a commitment to positive change and growth. It requires both partners to work together to mend the cracks, strengthen the bonds, and forge a new path of healing, forgiveness, and renewed trust.

Embracing Trust and Honesty as a Compass:

In the tumultuous seas of life and love, trust and honesty serve as the guiding compass that steers partners through storms and calms alike. They offer a sense of direction, security, and unity that transcends challenges and adversities. Embracing trust and honesty as guiding principles in a relationship cultivates a sense of emotional intimacy, authenticity, and connection that weathers the tests of time and strengthens the ties that bind partners in a shared journey of love and growth.

Trust and honesty are not just words but guiding principles that shape the very essence of a relationship. They form the resilient fibers that weave hearts together, minds aligned, and souls entwined in a dance of vulnerability, acceptance, and love. Nurture trust and honesty as the foundation of your bond, and watch as the roots deepen, the branches spread, and the blossoms of your connection bloom in the light of shared truth and unwavering faith in each other.

Trust and honesty are essential components of a healthy relationship. When both partners feel secure and supported, they can build a strong foundation for a lasting bond. In this chapter, we'll discuss how to build and maintain trust, how to be honest and transparent in your interactions, and how to forgive and move forward when mistakes are made.

CHAPTER 3: EMOTIONAL INTELLIGENCE - UNDERSTANDING AND MANAGING YOUR EMOTIONS

In the intricate tapestry of human experience, emotions stand as the vibrant hues that color our interactions, decisions, and relationships. Emotional intelligence, the ability to perceive, understand, and manage our own emotions, as well those of others, plays a pivotal role in shaping our mental well-being, resilience, and interpersonal dynamics. In this chapter, we explore the profound impact of emotional intelligence on our lives and relationships, delving into strategies for cultivating self-awareness, empathy, and emotional regulation.

The Essence of Emotional Intelligence:

Emotional intelligence encompasses a range of skills that enable us to navigate the complex landscape of emotions with wisdom and grace. It involves self-awareness, the ability to recognize and understand our own feelings; self-regulation, the capacity to manage our emotions and impulses effectively; empathy, the skill of sensing and understanding others' emotions; social skills, the proficiency in managing relationships and communicating effectively; and motivation, the drive to achieve personal and professional goals with resilience and determination. Together, these components form the foundation of emotional intelligence, empowering us to navigate the highs and lows of life with insight and resilience.

Self-Awareness - The Gateway to Emotional Intelligence:

Self-awareness serves as the cornerstone of emotional intelligence, offering a window into our inner world of thoughts, feelings, and beliefs. It involves tuning into our emotions, identifying their triggers, and understanding how they influence our thoughts and behaviors. Cultivating self-awareness requires introspection, mindfulness, and a willingness to explore our inner landscape with curiosity and compassion. By developing a deep understanding of our emotional patterns and responses, we gain greater control over our actions and choices, paving the way for emotional growth and self-empowerment.

Embracing Emotional Regulation:

Emotional regulation is the art of managing our emotions in a healthy and constructive manner, rather than being controlled by them. It involves recognizing and acknowledging our feelings, expressing them appropriately, and finding effective ways to cope with stress, anger, or sadness. Techniques such as deep breathing, mindfulness, journaling, and seeking support from loved ones can help us navigate emotional turmoil and maintain a sense of balance and composure. By honing our emotional regulation skills, we cultivate resilience, adaptability, and a sense of inner peace that empowers us to navigate life's challenges with grace and clarity.

Cultivating Empathy and Social Skills:

Empathy is the ability to step into another person's shoes, understand their emotions, and respond with compassion and care. It involves active listening, perspective-taking, and genuine concern for others' well-being. By cultivating empathy, we foster deeper connections, build trust, and strengthen our relationships with others. Social skills play a complementary role in emotional intelligence, enabling us to communicate effectively, resolve conflicts, and navigate complex social situations with finesse. By honing our social skills, we create a supportive and harmonious environment where understanding, respect, and collaboration thrive.

Motivation and Goal Setting:

Motivation is the driving force behind our actions and aspirations, propelling us to pursue our goals with passion and determination. Setting clear, achievable goals that align with our values and aspirations can fuel our motivation and enhance our sense of purpose and fulfillment. By leveraging our emotional intelligence to clarify our intentions, overcome obstacles, and stay focused on our objectives, we create a roadmap for personal and professional growth that reflects our deepest desires and aspirations.

Navigating Emotional Intelligence in Relationships:

In the context of relationships, emotional intelligence serves as a guiding light that illuminates the path to connection, understanding, and intimacy. By applying the principles of emotional intelligence - self-awareness, empathy, emotional regulation, and social skills - we foster harmonious and fulfilling relationships built on trust, authenticity, and mutual respect. By communicating honestly, listening empathetically, and navigating conflicts with grace and understanding, we create a space for emotional growth, connection, and shared vulnerability that strengthens the bonds between partners.

Strategies for Enhancing Emotional Intelligence:

1. Practice mindfulness and self-reflection to deepen self-awareness.

    2. Develop healthy coping mechanisms for managing emotions effectively.

    3. Cultivate empathy through active listening and perspective-

taking.

4. Enhance social skills through communication, conflict resolution, and collaboration.

5. Set goals that align with your values and aspirations to fuel motivation and drive.

Emotional intelligence is a transformative force that enriches our lives, relationships, and sense of well-being. By honing our self-awareness, embracing empathy, mastering emotional regulation, and nurturing social skills, we cultivate a profound understanding and management of our emotions that empowers us to navigate life's joys and challenges with grace, resilience, and authenticity. Embrace the journey of emotional intelligence as a path to self-discovery, growth, and connection that leads to a deeper sense of fulfillment, balance, and harmony within ourselves and our relationships.

Emotional intelligence is the ability to understand and manage your own emotions, as well as empathize with your partner's emotions. It's a crucial skill for building a strong and healthy relationship. In this chapter, we'll explore how to develop emotional intelligence, how to recognize and manage your emotions, and how to empathize with your partner's feelings.

CHAPTER 4: SUPPORT AND ENCOURAGEMENT - BEING A ROCK FOR YOUR PARTNER

In the sacred dance of relationships, the roles of support and encouragement are akin to the sturdy rocks that anchor us through life's storms and guide us towards calmer waters. Being a rock for your partner entails offering unwavering support, empathetic understanding, and uplifting encouragement in times of joy, challenge, and personal growth. In this chapter, we explore the transformative power of being a pillar of strength for your partner, nurturing a foundation of trust, resilience, and emotional connection within the relationship.

The Role of Support and Encouragement:

Support and encouragement form the bedrock of a healthy and fulfilling relationship, solidifying the bond between partners through mutual care, understanding, and validation. As a rock for your partner, you stand as a source of strength, comfort, and reassurance in the face of adversity, offering a steady hand and a compassionate heart to navigate life's highs and lows together. By fostering an environment of support and encouragement, you create a safe, nurturing space where vulnerability, growth, and shared aspirations can flourish.

Offering Unconditional Support:

Unconditional support involves being present for your partner in times of need, offering a listening ear, a comforting embrace, and a shoulder to lean on without judgment or conditions. It means standing by their side through challenges, celebrating their successes, and affirming their worth and resilience in the face of struggles. By demonstrating unwavering support, you create a sense of security and trust that fortifies the emotional connection and bond between partners, fostering a deep sense of acceptance, belonging, and love.

Empathetic Understanding:

Empathetic understanding is the ability to step into your partner's shoes, see the world through their eyes, and validate their feelings, experiences, and perspective with compassion and care. It involves active listening, non-judgmental communication, and genuine concern for your partner's emotional well-being. By cultivating empathetic understanding, you create a space of emotional safety, acceptance, and connection that nurtures trust, vulnerability, and intimacy within the relationship.

Uplifting Encouragement:

Uplifting encouragement involves offering words of affirmation, motivation, and positivity to inspire and empower your partner in moments of self-doubt, challenge, and growth. It entails acknowledging their strengths, celebrating their achievements, and reminding them of their resilience and potential to overcome obstacles with grace and determination. By providing uplifting encouragement, you instill a sense of confidence, belief, and self-worth in your partner, fueling their sense of motivation and purpose in pursuing their dreams and aspirations.

Celebrating Successes and Milestones:

As a rock for your partner, it is essential to celebrate their successes, milestones, and achievements, no matter how big or small. By sharing in their joys, triumphs, and moments of pride, you validate their efforts, affirm their value, and strengthen their sense of self-worth and accomplishment. Celebrating successes together fosters a spirit of joy, gratitude, and connection, enriching the emotional bond and shared experiences that define the relationship.

Weathering Storms and Uncertainties:

In the face of challenges, setbacks, and uncertainties, being a rock for your partner means offering unwavering support, patience, and understanding during times of struggle and adversity. It involves standing strong in the face of storms, providing a steady presence, and a calm demeanor that fosters a sense of stability, hope, and resilience. By weathering challenges together, you strengthen the bond, deepen the trust, and forge a path of growth, healing, and shared strength that guides you through life's uncertainties and trials.

Navigating Personal Growth and Change:

As individuals evolve and grow, being a rock for your partner entails navigating the journey of personal growth and change with empathy, patience, and open-hearted acceptance. It involves supporting their aspirations, encouraging their self-discovery, and embracing their evolving identity with love and understanding. By navigating personal growth and change together, you create a space of mutual respect, authenticity, and compassion that allows both partners to thrive, transform, and flourish in their individual journeys and shared path as a couple.

Strategies for Being a Rock for Your Partner:

1. Practice active listening and empathetic understanding in your communication with your partner.

2. Offer unwavering support, comfort, and encouragement in times of need and adversity.

3. Celebrate your partner's successes, milestones, and achievements with genuine joy and pride.

4. Nurture a sense of emotional safety, acceptance,

and vulnerability in your relationship through open, honest communication.

5. Navigate personal growth and change together with empathy, patience, and love, fostering a spirit of shared evolution and mutual respect.

Being a rock for your partner is a transformative journey of connection, growth, and love, where you stand as a pillar of strength, support, and encouragement in times of joy, challenge, and personal evolution. By cultivating a space of empathy, trust, and vulnerability, you create a foundation of resilience, intimacy, and emotional connection that weathers the tests of time and strengthens the bond between partners in a relationship defined by care, compassion, and unwavering commitment to each other's well-being and happiness. Embrace the role of being a rock for your partner with love, grace, and understanding, and watch as your connection deepens, your hearts align, and your shared journey of growth, love, and authenticity unfolds in the light of mutual trust, encouragement, and enduring love.

Being a supportive partner is essential for building a strong and healthy relationship. When both partners feel encouraged and supported, they can pursue their goals and dreams with confidence. In this chapter, we'll discuss how to be a supportive partner, how to encourage personal growth and development, and how to celebrate each other's successes.

: **Chapter 5: Intimacy and Connection - Building a Strong Physical and Emotional Bond**

In the intricate dance of relationships, intimacy and connection stand as the radiant threads that weave hearts, minds, and souls together in a tapestry of love, trust, and shared vulnerability. Building a strong physical and emotional bond with your partner entails nurturing a deep sense of closeness, understanding, and emotional resonance that transcends barriers and fosters a profound sense of connection and unity. In this chapter, we explore the transformative power of intimacy and connection in shaping the emotional landscape of a relationship, delving into strategies for cultivating physical and emotional closeness, vulnerability, and authenticity in the journey of love and partnership.

The Essence of Intimacy and Connection:

Intimacy and connection form the heart of a meaningful and fulfilling relationship, encapsulating a sense of closeness, trust, and shared vulnerability between partners. Intimacy encompasses emotional, physical, and spiritual closeness, fostering a sense of resonance, understanding, and acceptance that binds hearts in a dance of love, compassion, and authenticity. In the realm of connection, partners forge a bond of shared experiences, memories, and aspirations that deepen their emotional connection and nurture a sense of belonging, support, and mutual growth within the relationship.

Navigating Emotional Intimacy:

Emotional intimacy involves opening your heart, sharing your thoughts, feelings, and vulnerabilities, and creating a space of trust and understanding where partners can express their true selves freely and authentically. It entails active listening, empathy, and a willingness to be vulnerable and transparent about your emotions, fears, and desires. Cultivating emotional intimacy requires patience, empathy, and a commitment to deepening the bond of trust and acceptance that allows partners to feel seen, heard, and valued in their truest essence.

Incorporating Physical Intimacy:

Physical intimacy encompasses a range of expressions of love, desire, and closeness, from holding hands and cuddling to sexual intimacy and shared physical experiences that deepen the bond between partners. It involves communication, consent, and a mutual understanding of each other's needs, boundaries, and desires. Physical intimacy fosters a sense of connection, passion, and joy that enriches the emotional landscape of the relationship, creating a space of tenderness, passion, and shared pleasure that reflects the depth of love and connection between partners.

Sharing Vulnerability and Trust:

Vulnerability is the key to unlocking the depths of emotional intimacy and connection in a relationship, allowing partners to let down their guard, share their fears, and reveal their true selves with authenticity and courage. It involves stepping into the unknown, embracing uncertainty, and trusting your partner to hold space for your vulnerabilities with compassion and care. By sharing vulnerability and building trust, partners create a space of acceptance, empathy, and unconditional love that nourishes the roots of connection and intimacy, fostering a sense of security, acceptance, and mutual understanding within the relationship.

Nurturing Communication and Understanding:

Effective communication serves as the bridge that connects partners in the realm of connection and intimacy, fostering a deep sense of understanding, empathy, and resonance between hearts and minds. It involves active listening, empathy, and a willingness to engage in honest, open dialogue about your feelings, needs, and desires. By nurturing communication and understanding, partners create a space of emotional safety, acceptance, and vulnerability that allows for shared experiences, growth, and transformation within the relationship.

Practicing Presence and Appreciation:

Presence and appreciation are the cornerstones of building a strong physical and emotional bond, inviting partners to be fully engaged, attentive, and mindful in their interactions and shared experiences. Presence involves being fully present in the moment, offering your undivided attention, and creating a space of connection that transcends distractions and external pressures.

Appreciation entails recognizing and celebrating the beauty, uniqueness, and value of your partner, showing gratitude, and expressing love in words and actions that reflect the depth of your connection and bond.

Exploring Shared Experiences and Memories:

Shared experiences and memories form the tapestry of connection and intimacy, weaving a narrative of love, growth, and resilience that defines the relationship. By exploring new adventures, creating meaningful rituals, and cherishing shared moments together, partners deepen their emotional connection, strengthen their bond, and nurture a sense of partnership, unity, and shared vision that guides them through life's joys and challenges as a team.

Strategies for Building Intimacy and Connection:

1. Cultivate emotional intimacy through open, honest communication and vulnerability.
2. Foster physical intimacy through shared experiences, affection, and physical touch.
3. Share vulnerability and build trust by embracing authenticity and courage in revealing your true self.
4. Nurture communication and understanding through active listening, empathy, and honest dialogue.
5. Practice presence, appreciation, and gratitude to create a space of love, connection, and emotional resonance.
6. Explore shared experiences and create memories that deepen emotional connection and strengthen the bond between partners.

Building a strong physical and emotional bond with your partner is a transformative journey of love, trust, and shared vulnerability, where hearts intertwine, minds align, and souls resonate in a dance of connection, intimacy, and authenticity. By cultivating emotional and physical closeness, vulnerability, and mutual understanding, partners create a space of trust, acceptance, and unconditional love that anchors them through life's highs and lows, shaping a relationship defined by resilience, intimacy, and unwavering commitment to each other's well-being and happiness. Embrace the journey of intimacy and connection with love, courage, and openness, and watch as your bond deepens, your hearts align, and your shared path of growth, love, and connection unfolds in the light of trust, vulnerability, and enduring love.

Intimacy and connection are vital components of a healthy relationship. When both partners feel physically and emotionally connected, they can build a strong and lasting bond. In this chapter, we'll explore how to build a strong physical and emotional connection, how to prioritize quality time together, and how to keep the spark going in a growing union.

CHAPTER 5: INTIMACY AND CONNECTION - BUILDING A STRONG PHYSICAL AND EMOTIONAL BOND

Intimacy and connection stand as the radiant threads that weave hearts, minds, and souls together in a tapestry of love, trust, and shared vulnerability. Building a strong physical and emotional bond with your partner entails nurturing a deep sense of closeness, understanding, and emotional resonance that transcends barriers and fosters a profound sense of connection and unity. In this chapter, we explore the transformative power of intimacy and connection in shaping the emotional landscape of a relationship, delving into strategies for cultivating physical and emotional closeness, vulnerability, and authenticity in the journey of love and partnership.

The Essence of Intimacy and Connection:

Intimacy and connection form the heart of a meaningful and fulfilling relationship, encapsulating a sense of closeness, trust, and shared vulnerability between partners. Intimacy encompasses emotional, physical, and spiritual closeness, fostering a sense of resonance, understanding, and acceptance that binds hearts in a dance of love, compassion, and authenticity. In the realm of connection, partners forge a bond of shared experiences, memories, and aspirations that deepen their emotional connection and nurture a sense of belonging, support, and mutual growth within the relationship.

Navigating Emotional Intimacy:

Emotional intimacy involves opening your heart, sharing your thoughts, feelings, and vulnerabilities, and creating a space of trust and understanding where partners can express their true selves freely and authentically. It entails active listening, empathy, and a willingness to be vulnerable and transparent about your emotions, fears, and desires. Cultivating emotional intimacy requires patience, empathy, and a commitment to deepening the bond of trust and acceptance that allows partners to feel seen, heard, and valued in their truest essence.

Incorporating Physical Intimacy:

Physical intimacy encompasses a range of expressions of love, desire, and closeness, from holding hands and cuddling to sexual intimacy and shared physical experiences that deepen the bond between partners. It involves communication, consent, and a mutual understanding of each other's needs, boundaries, and desires. Physical intimacy fosters a sense of connection, passion, and joy that enriches the emotional landscape of the relationship, creating a space of tenderness, passion, and shared pleasure that reflects the depth of love and connection between partners.

Sharing Vulnerability and Trust:

Vulnerability is the key to unlocking the depths of emotional intimacy and connection in a relationship, allowing partners to let down their guard, share their fears, and reveal their true selves with authenticity and courage. It involves stepping into the unknown, embracing uncertainty, and trusting your partner to hold space for your vulnerabilities with compassion and care. By sharing vulnerability and building trust, partners create a space of acceptance, empathy, and unconditional love that nourishes the roots of connection and intimacy, fostering a sense of security, acceptance, and mutual understanding within the relationship.

Nurturing Communication and Understanding:

Effective communication serves as the bridge that connects partners in the realm of connection and intimacy, fostering a deep sense of understanding, empathy, and resonance between hearts and minds. It involves active listening, empathy, and a willingness to engage in honest, open dialogue about your feelings, needs, and desires. By nurturing communication and understanding, partners create a space of emotional safety, acceptance, and vulnerability that allows for shared experiences, growth, and transformation within the relationship.

Practicing Presence and Appreciation:

Presence and appreciation are the cornerstones of building a strong physical and emotional bond, inviting partners to be fully engaged, attentive, and mindful in their interactions and shared experiences. Presence involves being fully present in the moment, offering your undivided attention, and creating a space of connection that transcends distractions and external pressures. Appreciation entails recognizing and celebrating the beauty, uniqueness, and value of your partner, showing gratitude, and expressing love in words and actions that reflect the depth of your connection and bond.

Exploring Shared Experiences and Memories:

Shared experiences and memories form the tapestry of connection and intimacy, weaving a narrative of love, growth, and resilience that defines the relationship. By exploring new adventures, creating meaningful rituals, and cherishing shared moments together, partners deepen their emotional connection, strengthen their bond, and nurture a sense of partnership, unity, and shared vision that guides them through life's joys and challenges as a team.

Strategies for Building Intimacy and Connection:

1. Cultivate emotional intimacy through open, honest communication and vulnerability.
2. Foster physical intimacy through shared experiences, affection, and physical touch.
3. Share vulnerability and build trust by embracing authenticity and courage in revealing your true self.
4. Nurture communication and understanding through active listening, empathy, and honest dialogue.
5. Practice presence, appreciation, and gratitude to create a space of love, connection, and emotional resonance.
6. Explore shared experiences and create memories that deepen emotional connection and strengthen the bond between partners.

Building a strong physical and emotional bond with your partner is a transformative journey of love, trust, and shared vulnerability, where hearts intertwine, minds align, and souls resonate in a dance of connection, intimacy, and authenticity. By cultivating emotional and physical closeness, vulnerability, and mutual understanding, partners create a space of trust, acceptance, and unconditional love that anchors them through life's highs and lows, shaping a relationship defined by resilience, intimacy, and unwavering commitment to each other's well-being and happiness. Embrace the journey of intimacy and connection with love, courage, and openness, and watch as your bond deepens, your hearts align, and your shared path of growth, love, and connection unfolds in the light of trust, vulnerability, and enduring love.

Intimacy and connection are vital components of a healthy relationship. When both partners feel physically and emotionally connected, they can build a strong and lasting bond. In this chapter, we'll explore how to build a strong physical and emotional connection, how to prioritize quality time together, and how to keep the spark.

CHAPTER 6: INDEPENDENCE AND INTERDEPENDENCE - FINDING A HEALTHY BALANCE

In the world of relationships, the delicate dance between independence and interdependence forms the foundation of a healthy, thriving partnership. Balancing individual autonomy, self-reliance and shared connection and support, partners navigate the nuances of personal growth, intimacy, and mutual respect that define a strong and resilient bond. In this chapter, we explore the transformative power of finding a healthy equilibrium between independence and interdependence in fostering a relationship built on trust, respect, and shared growthEmbracing Independence:

Independence is the art of cultivating a sense of self-sufficiency, autonomy, and agency within the context of a relationship. It involves honoring your individuality, values, and aspirations, and pursuing personal growth, passions, and aspirations that align with your authentic self. Embracing independence means fostering a sense of self-worth, resilience, and empowerment that allows you to navigate life's challenges and triumphs with confidence, authenticity, and purpose.

Nurturing Interdependence:

Interdependence is the synergy between partners that fosters a mutual reliance, support, and connection in navigating life's journey together. It involves acknowledging the strengths, vulnerabilities, and needs of each partner, and co-creating a space of shared responsibility, trust, and collaboration that deepens the bond and fosters a sense of unity and partnership. By nurturing interdependence, partners cultivate a foundation of trust, acceptance, and empowerment that allows for shared growth, collaboration, and resilience in the face of life's joys and challenges.

Finding Balance Between Independence and Interdependence:

Balance between independence and interdependence lies in navigating the dynamic dance between honoring your individuality and supporting your partner's needs and aspirations. It involves holding space for autonomy, self-expression, and personal growth, while fostering a sense of connection, intimacy, and shared vision that aligns with the values and aspirations of both partners. Finding balance requires open communication, empathy, and a willingness to embrace vulnerability, acceptance, and mutual respect in navigating the complexities of a partnership built on trust, authenticity, and unwavering commitment to each other's well-being and happiness.

Strategies for Cultivating a Healthy Balance:

1. **Prioritize Self-Care**: Dedicate time for self-reflection, self-care practices, and nurturing your physical, emotional, and mental well-being as an individual.

2. **Communicate Openly**: Foster open, honest communication with your partner about your needs, boundaries, and aspirations, and create a space for shared dialogue and understanding.

3. **Set Boundaries**: Establish clear boundaries that honor your individual needs, desires, and values, while respecting and supporting your partner's autonomy and personal growth.

4. **Practice Empathy**: Cultivate empathy, active listening,

and understanding in your interactions with your partner, acknowledging their feelings, needs, and perspectives with care and compassion.

5. **Collaborate and Support**: Embrace collaboration and support in your shared experiences, projects, and aspirations, fostering a sense of shared responsibility, trust, and unity as partners navigating life's journey together.

Embracing Growth and Evolution:

Independence and interdependence invite partners to embrace growth, evolution, and transformation as individuals and as a couple. By honoring your unique strengths, vulnerabilities, and aspirations, while fostering a sense of shared vision, connection, and partnership, you create a space of mutual support, trust, and emotional resonance that guides you through life's joys and challenges with grace, authenticity, and unwavering commitment to each other's well-being and happiness. Embrace the journey of finding a healthy balance between independence and interdependence with love, courage, and openness, and watch as your bond deepens, your hearts align, and your shared path of growth, love, and connection unfolds in the light of trust, respect, and enduring love.

Navigating the delicate balance between independence and interdependence is a transformative journey of self-discovery, partnership, and shared growth, where partners cultivate a sense of autonomy, unity, and collaboration that honors the individuality and |

Independence and interdependence are both essential components of a healthy relationship. When both partners maintain their own identity and autonomy, while also being supportive and dependent on each other, they can build a strong and balanced relationship. In this chapter, we'll discuss how to maintain your own identity and autonomy, how to balance independence and interdependence, and how to support each other's goals and aspirations.

△△△

CHAPTER 7: CONFLICT AND RESOLUTION - ADDRESSING CONFLICTS IN A HEALTHY AND CONSTRUCTIVE MANNER

Conflict is an inherent part of any relationship, a natural reflection of differing perspectives, values, and needs that arise when two individuals come together. However, how partners navigate conflict can either strengthen the bond between them or erode the foundation of trust and understanding. In this chapter, we explore strategies for addressing conflicts in a healthy and constructive manner, fostering communication, empathy, and resolution to deepen the connection and trust within a relationship.

Understanding Conflict:

Conflict is not inherently negative but rather an opportunity for growth, understanding, and deeper connection between partners. It arises from differing viewpoints, unmet needs, and miscommunications that can lead to tension, frustration, and emotional distress. By viewing conflict as a natural part of the relationship journey, partners can approach it with curiosity, empathy, and a willingness to engage in open, honest dialogue to address underlying issues and foster resolution.

Effective Communication in Conflict:

Communication serves as the foundation for addressing conflicts in a healthy and constructive manner. It involves active listening, empathy, and a willingness to understand your partner's perspective, feelings, and needs. By fostering open, honest dialogue, expressing your thoughts and emotions with clarity and respect, and seeking to understand rather than blame, partners create a space of mutual respect, understanding, and validation that paves the way for productive conflict resolution.

Embracing Empathy and Understanding:

Empathy is the key to bridging the gap between differing viewpoints and fostering connection and understanding in times of conflict. It involves stepping into your partner's shoes, recognizing their feelings, and responding with compassion and care. By practicing active listening, perspective-taking, and non-judgmental communication, partners can cultivate empathy, validate each other's emotions, and create a sense of emotional safety, acceptance, and vulnerability that nurtures trust and understanding within the relationship.

Finding Common Ground and Solutions:

Conflict resolution entails finding common ground, seeking compromise, and generating mutually beneficial solutions that meet the needs and values of both partners. It involves focusing on shared goals, interests, and values, acknowledging each other's perspectives, and working collaboratively towards resolution. By fostering a spirit of cooperation, empathy, and respect, partners can navigate conflicts with grace, understanding, and a shared commitment to finding positive outcomes that strengthen the bond and trust between them.

Healthy Conflict Resolution Strategies:

1. Practice active listening and empathetic understanding to validate your partner's emotions and perspectives.
    2. Express your thoughts and feelings with clarity, honesty,

and respect, fostering open communication.

3. Seek to understand your partner's needs and values, focusing on finding common ground and shared solutions.

4. Approach conflicts with a mindset of curiosity, empathy, and willingness to engage in constructive dialogue.

5. Embrace compromise, seeking mutually beneficial solutions that honor both partners' perspectives and needs.

Navigating Emotional Triggers and Reactions:

During conflict, partners may experience emotional triggers that activate past hurts, fears, and insecurities. It is essential to recognize and acknowledge these triggers, communicate them with your partner, and work together to navigate them with compassion, empathy, and understanding. By addressing emotional reactions with mindfulness and vulnerability, partners can deepen their connection, validate each other's feelings, and strengthen the emotional bond within the relationship.

Cultivating Forgiveness and Healing:

Conflict resolution often involves forgiveness, healing, and a willingness to let go of past grievances in order to move forward with trust, understanding, and connection. By practicing forgiveness, partners release resentment, foster emotional growth, and create space for healing and renewal within the relationship. It involves acknowledging the pain, seeking reconciliation, and allowing space for vulnerability, compassion, and mutual growth that transforms conflicts into opportunities for deeper connection and understanding.

The Role of Healthy Boundaries:

Healthy boundaries play a crucial role in conflict resolution, establishing guidelines, respect, and self-care that foster clear communication, emotional safety, and trust within the relationship. By setting and communicating boundaries, partners create a space of respect, autonomy, and personal well-being that nurtures a sense of emotional safety, acceptance, and mutual understanding in times of conflict. Boundaries provide a roadmap for resolving conflicts with grace and respect, honoring each other's needs, values, and perspectives as they navigate the complexities of the relationship journey together.

Strategies for Conflict Resolution:

1. Practice active listening, empathy, and non-judgmental communication in conflict.
2. Express thoughts and emotions with clarity, honesty, and respect, fostering open dialogue.
3. Seek common ground and solutions that meet the needs and values of both partners.
4. Address emotional triggers and reactions with mindfulness, vulnerability, and understanding.
5. Cultivate forgiveness, healing, and a willingness to let go of past grievances for mutual growth and connection.
6. Establish healthy boundaries that foster clear communication, respect, and emotional safety during conflicts.

Conflict is an opportunity for growth, understanding, and deeper connection between partners. By embracing conflicts with curiosity, empathy, and a commitment to constructive communication and resolution, partners can navigate challenges with grace, compassion, and understanding that deepens the emotional bond and trust within the relationship. Viewed through the lens of growth, conflict can serve as a catalyst for self-awareness, mutual understanding, and shared growth that strengthens the foundation of love, trust, and resilience between partners on their journey of connection, understanding, and harmony. Embrace conflict as a path to deeper understanding, compassion, and connection, and watch as your relationship flourishes in the light of constructive communication, empathy, and shared vulnerability.

Conflicts are a natural part of any relationship. However, it's how you address and resolve conflicts that can make or break the relationship. In this chapter, we'll explore how to address conflicts in a healthy and constructive manner, how to find common ground and compromise, and how to seek outside help when needed.

△△△

CHAPTER 8: PERSONAL GROWTH AND DEVELOPMENT - CONTINUING TO GROW AND EVOLVE AS INDIVIDUALS

In the journey of life and relationships, personal growth and development stand as the guiding lights that illuminate the path to self-discovery, fulfillment, and transformation. As individuals, we are perpetual works in progress, navigating the complexities of self-discovery, learning, and evolution with courage, openness, and resilience. In this chapter, we explore the transformative power of personal growth and development, delving into strategies for cultivating self-awareness, embracing change, and nurturing a sense of purpose and authenticity in the journey of personal evolution and growth.

The Essence of Personal Growth and Development:

Personal growth and development entail a continuous process of self-exploration, learning, and adaptation that propels us towards higher levels of self-awareness, fulfillment, and authenticity. It involves expanding our horizons, challenging our beliefs, and stepping outside our comfort zone to embrace change, uncertainty, and personal transformation. By cultivating a spirit of curiosity, openness, and courage, we embark on a journey of personal growth that deepens our understanding of ourselves, expands our capacities, and shapes our identity in alignment with our values, aspirations, and purpose in life.

Self-Awareness - The Gateway to Personal Growth:

Self-awareness is the foundational pillar of personal growth and development, offering a mirror into our thoughts, emotions, and behaviors that fosters a deep understanding of our strengths, weaknesses, and aspirations. It involves introspection, mindfulness, and a willingness to explore our inner landscape with curiosity and compassion, uncovering layers of our identity, beliefs, and desires that shape our sense of self and guide our choices and actions. By cultivating self-awareness, we gain clarity, insight, and direction in our journey of personal growth, empowering us to navigate life's challenges, triumphs, and uncertainties with grace, resilience, and purpose.

Embracing Change and Adaptation:

Change is an inevitable part of the human experience, inviting us to embrace impermanence, opportunity, and growth as catalysts for personal evolution and transformation. It involves letting go of old patterns, beliefs, and limitations that no longer serve us, and opening ourselves to new experiences, perspectives, and possibilities that expand our horizons and enrich our lives. By embracing change with an open heart and a curious mind, we invite personal growth, adaptation, and renewal into our lives, nurturing a spirit of resilience, flexibility, and growth that empowers us to thrive in the face of life's inevitable transitions and transformations.

Setting Goals and Aspirations:

Setting goals and aspirations is a powerful tool for personal growth and development, providing a roadmap that guides us towards our dreams, aspirations, and authentic desires in life. It involves clarifying our intentions, identifying our values, and envisioning our ideal future self, then breaking down our aspirations into actionable steps, cultivating a sense of direction, purpose, and motivation that propels us towards personal evolution and growth. By setting meaningful, achievable goals that resonate with our values and aspirations, we create a framework for personal growth that reflects our deepest desires, strengths, and potential, nourishing a sense of fulfillment, purpose, and authenticity that guides us towards a life of meaning, joy, and self-actualization.

Cultivating Resilience and Adaptability:

Resilience and adaptability are essential qualities that underpin personal growth and development, enabling us to navigate life's challenges, setbacks, and uncertainties with courage, grace, and fortitude. Resilience involves bouncing back from adversity, learning from failures, and embracing setbacks as opportunities for growth and discovery. Adaptability entails embracing change, uncertainty, and complexity with an open mind and a willingness to innovate, evolve, and thrive in the face of change and transformation. By cultivating resilience and adaptability, we foster a sense of inner strength, flexibility, and empowerment that equips us to face life's uncertainties with courage, resilience, and a growth mindset that fosters personal evolution and transformation.

The Power of Lifelong Learning and Self-Discovery:

Lifelong learning and self-discovery are the vehicles that propel us on a journey of personal growth and development, inviting us to explore new horizons, expand our knowledge, and deepen our understanding of ourselves and the world around us. It involves curiosity, exploration, and a thirst for knowledge that fuels our intellectual, emotional, and spiritual growth, fostering a sense of wonder, discovery, and transformation that enriches our lives and nurtures our personal evolution. By embracing lifelong learning and self-discovery as essential components of personal growth, we unlock the door to new ideas, perspectives, and possibilities that inspire us to evolve, adapt, and flourish as individuals, partners, and global citizens in a world of constant change and transformation.

Nurturing Personal Growth in Relationships:

Personal growth and development are interwoven with the fabric of relationships, offering us mirrors, challenges, and opportunities for self-discovery, learning, and transformation through our interactions with others. In the context of relationships, personal growth entails supporting each other's aspirations, respecting individual boundaries, and encouraging each other's self-discovery and evolution with empathy, love, and acceptance. By nurturing personal growth within relationships, partners create a space of mutual respect, understanding, and support that empowers each other to evolve, lead, and thrive as individuals united in a journey of love, growth, and shared transformation that enriches their connection, partnership, and personal development.

Strategies for Personal Growth and Development:

1. Cultivate self-awareness through mindfulness, reflection, and self-exploration.

2. Embrace change and adaptation as opportunities for growth, learning, and transformation.

3. Set goals and aspirations that align with your values, dreams, and authentic desires.

4. Cultivate resilience and adaptability by embracing setbacks, challenges, and uncertainties as opportunities for learning and growth.

5. Embrace lifelong learning and self-discovery to deepen your knowledge, understanding, and perspective on yourself and the world around you.

6. Nurture personal growth within relationships by supporting each other's aspirations, fostering trust, and encouraging each other's journeys of self-discovery and evolution with empathy, love, and acceptance.

Personal growth and development are transformative journeys of self-discovery, learning, and evolution that empower us to deepen our self-awareness, expand our horizons, and cultivate a sense of purpose, fulfillment, and authenticity. By embracing change, setting goals, nurturing resilience, and fostering a spirit of lifelong learning and self-discovery, we embark on a path of personal growth that leads us towards the fullest expression of our potential, values, and aspirations in life. Embrace the journey of personal growth and development with courage, openness, and curiosity, and watch as you evolve, adapt, and flourish as individuals on a path of self-discovery, meaning, and transformation that guides you towards a life of fulfillment, growth, and purpose.

Personal growth and development are essential components of a healthy relationship. When both partners continue to grow and evolve as individuals, they can bring new experiences and perspectives to the relationship. In this chapter, we'll discuss how to continue growing and evolving as individuals, how to support each other's personal growth, and how to embrace change and new experiences.

△△△

Conclusion

Building a healthy relationship takes effort and commitment from both partners. By prioritizing communication, trust, and mutual respect, you can create a strong bond that can withstand life's challenges. Remember to always support each other's growth and development, and to address conflicts in a healthy and constructive manner. With these tips and strategies, you can build a lasting and fulfilling relationship.

ACKNOWLEDGEMENT

I Would Like To Express My Deep Gratitude To My Family Friends For Their Unwavering Support And Encouragement Throughout This Journey. Special Acknowlegement To My Brother And His Wife For All Those Convos I Had A Plan This Whole Time Lol.

Special Thanks To My Partner, Who Has Been My Rock And Source Of Energy Needed For This Project I Love You . Your Love And Belief In Me Have Made This Book Possible. Can't Forget My Kids Who Has Been My Biggest Inspiration To Make This Happen!!!!!!

Heartfelt thanks to all the readers and followers who have shown interest in my work and motivated me to share my insights on building healthy and lasting relationships. I appreciate the valuable feedback and constructive criticism provided by my beta readers and mentors, helping me refine and improve the contents of this book.

Last but not least, I want to thank the lord Jesus Christ for guiding me on this path of self-discovery and personal growth, allowing me to spread love and positivity through my writing. Amen

AFTERWORD

As You Reach The End Of This Book, I Hope You Have Found Valuable Insights And Practical Tips To Nurture And Strengthen Your Relationship. Remember, The Journey To A Successful Partnership Is Ongoing And Requires Continuous Effort And Commitment From Both Parties.

Communication, Respect, And Understanding Are The Cornerstones Of A Healthy And Fulfilling Relationship. Embrace The Challenges As Opportunities For Growth And Learning, And Always Strive To Support And Uplift Each Other In Love.

I Encourage You To Reflect On The Principles Shared In This Book And Apply Them To Your Own Relationship Journey. May Your Bond Flourish, Your Love Deepen, And Your Happiness Know No Bounds.

Thank You For Allowing Me To Be A Part Of Your

Quest For A Lasting And Meaningful Connection. Wishing You Love, Joy, And Abundance In Your Relationship.

With Warmest Regards,

Otis Jackson Sr

ABOUT THE AUTHOR

Otis Jackson Sr

Otis Jackson Sr is the CEO of First Klass Ent LLC, a prominent entertainment business. Born in Portsmouth, VA, and raised in Petersburg, VA, Otis's upbringing in a single-parent home in the tough streets of Petersburg instilled in him resilience and determination. Overcoming numerous trials and tribulations, including a 5-year stint in federal prison, dealing with multiple woman and having 7 kids in the process while indulgin in the street life. He used these experiences to catalyze positive change in his life. It was during his time behind bars that he discovered his passion reading books and began honing his skills as a writer. Now, Mr Jackson is back and more determined than ever to make his mark in the world of music and literature, ready to conquer new horizons with a vengeance.

Otis Jackson Sr has faced life-altering challenges that have shaped his journey. In 2020, a harrowing encounter with a tractor-trailer nearly cost him his life, serving as a poignant reminder of life's fragility. This near-death experience ignited a newfound sense of purpose in Otis, propelling him to seize each moment with unwavering. Harnessing his passion for writing, Otis channeled his resilience into his craft, resulting in over 7 albums available on Apple Music and the ongoing creation of 3 captivating books. Despite the adversities he has encountered, Otis Jackson

Sr stands as a testament to the power of perseverance and the unwavering pursuit of artistic expression. Recently becoming a " PEER RECOVERY SPECIALIST" advocating for those suffering from substance abuse and mental health issues. Stepping into the mental health field he seems to be a jack of all trades with much more to come.

Made in the USA
Middletown, DE
10 June 2024

55410666R00031